When Tears Turn to Rain

IdnAc

LifeRich PUBLISHING

LifeRich Publishing is a registered trademark of The Reader's Digest Association, Inc.

LifeRich Publishing books may be ordered through booksellers or by contacting:

LifeRich Publishing
1663 Liberty Drive
Bloomington, IN 47403
www.liferichpublishing.com
1 (888) 238-8637

ISBN: 978-1-4897-0630-0 (sc)
ISBN: 978-1-4897-0631-7 (e)

Library of Congress Control Number: 2015920064

Print information available on the last page.

LifeRich Publishing rev. date: 12/04/2015

When Tears Turn to Rain
(A Journey into Sobriety)

This book is about a girl who drank herself into a
woman and only looked forward to death.

Share her journey into sobriety and her struggles along the
way. Broken, beat down, and dying, she makes a decision
to get sober. This is her story in her own words.

To my family:
I'm sorry you never got to know me, but I'm grateful you can
finally have that chance. I thank you all for never leaving my side.

To my children:
I will do my best to make up for lost time.
I'm truly sorry.

The Prison

In 2013, I simply existed. Hidden from reality, I pondered the what-ifs in my life.

I had emerged from behind a dark curtain and into a world not known by most. My existence diminished as the continuous poison of alcohol ran through my veins. Daily, I ingested the very thing that melted my mind.

Was I delusional? Yes. Crazy? Maybe. Shattered dreams had angered my very being. I zombie-walked among others in a state of coma. I answered questions with a blank stare. People left bewildered as did I.

Isolation was my best friend. Just the thought of conversation caused me distress. Solitude engulfed my every word when I was able to muster the courage to speak. In a room, I sat dazed and puzzled. The days ran into months and the months into years.

During the day, I sat among grim reapers. At night, I danced with movie stars. My Technicolor sci-fi dreams seemed to run into reality. I hoped for the worst, yet feared the best. With my yesterdays forgotten, my memories perished.

As the walls closed in on me, alcohol became my ultimate prison. I had sealed my own fate. Thankfully, this is not where my story ends.

This is where it begins.

Skid Row

I was eleven when tragedy struck twice. First, my father passed. Then, for the next year, a family member took advantage of me.

I was stripped of my dignity, self-worth, and childhood. With two tragedies that struck back-to-back, my mind shut down. I became a patient in the state mental hospital and wasn't released until I was fourteen.

Without proper mental help, it seemed, I was doomed from the start. And being separated from my mom and four brothers, I felt as though I faced the world alone.

The Journey

I was only fourteen when I got on my bicycle and headed for Skid Row. Although I didn't know it at the time, it would take a very, long time to get there.

First, I stopped at the Honesty shop, but it was too expensive. Besides, the line seemed miles long.

Around the corner, I found the liar store where one could buy one million lies for a penny. I bought the whole box and started using them right away.

I thought I would never run out of lies on my journey. I had used them on everyone I had encountered. I had used them on family, friends, boyfriends, and everyone in between.

I found a nice, cozy apartment on Party Court and lived there for about five years. During a period of a year and a half, I also visited my neighbor, cocaine—until the day I ended up in the hospital.

I turned my back on drugs, and moved to Alcoholic Avenue. I felt at home here. I decided to have to have a child here, and so I did.

For ten years, I never moved too far from Alcoholic Avenue. I had more children and lost them down the road. When I did move, I found a duplex on Self-Centered Street. I had been dancing for quite some time by now and used every man I met. This is where my dream of ever finding love fell to pieces.

By this time, my box of lies was getting empty, so I bought a box of one million more. I found new friends here: anger, worthlessness, and hate. They went everywhere with me and helped me use and abuse everyone in my path of destruction.

I hated the world—and everyone knew it. I stole, cheated, lied, hit people, hurt people, and hated myself. I moved again, and this time, I ended up on Memory Lane. Ironically, I lost my memory.

Now, I am not so sure I want it back.

I landed on Self-pity Street and used a lot more of my lies to get alcohol from friends, family, and acquaintances. When those supplies ran out, I found new people to use. I gambled and drank away every dollar I ever made.

I didn't work very much, but that was nothing new. Throughout my life, I could never hold down a job. At the age of forty, I realized that my journey was coming to an end. By this time, I was sick and shook so badly that I should have been hospitalized. But still determined to reach my destination of Skid Row, I pedaled all the harder.

In December 2012, one block before I reached Skid Row, I noticed a beautiful sign that was lit up with sunshine. Its two words were the most beautiful I had ever seen: Sobriety Place.

I got off my bicycle and looked back. Skid Row looked dark, lonely, scary, and empty. I left my bicycle and walked to Sobriety Place just to the right of Skid Row.

Although that was December 2012, I didn't take up residence in Sobriety Place until March 2013. I love it here; I would like to buy a house here sometime. But for now, I am simply taking it one day at a time.

I will make amends to those I have hurt on my journey. May we all find peace throughout our stay in Sobriety Place.

The Decision

Throughout my life, I have made hundreds of failed attempts to get sober. I had practically given up. I am a true alcoholic; I cannot recall very many days when I didn't drink.

At the age of fourty, I was at my wits' end. Chilled by the realization that death was just around the corner, I decided to get sober.

Desperate, I picked up the phone. After days on the phone with help lines, I finally found a sober program that would take me.

This is my story to the best of my recollection. With the help of journals that I kept, as well as memories shared from friends and family, I can take you on my journey into sobriety.

First, I wrote myself a reassuring note to read the next morning. The note explained that I couldn't go on like this anymore. I reminded myself that I was dying. I promised myself that I wanted to get sober. I told myself not to look back. I warned myself that there was no hope other than complete abstinence from alcohol.

When I woke up the next morning, I noticed that someone had packed a duffle bag and put a note on top of it. Hung over and nauseated, I stumbled to the bathroom as my head pounded. When I returned from the bathroom, I sat down on my bed and read the note.

Somehow, I remembered that I had made the decision to get sober when I wrote that note. I picked it up and read it again and again.

To stop shaking, I stumbled to the kitchen to get a beer. I mentioned to the people who lived in the flop house with me that I was leaving. I also explained that I was going to go downtown to get sober. I asked if someone might go with me. I waited for someone to speak up; no one volunteered.

After finishing my beer, I headed to the shower. Then I dressed, grabbed my bag, and said my good-byes. One man said, "Here is ten bucks; go get yourself a drink and come home in a better mood."

I took the money and explained that it wouldn't be spent on alcohol. When I thanked him for the bus fare, he laughed and said, "You'll be back."

And so, grasping my bag in hand, I walked out the front door as tears ran down my cheeks.

To get to the clinic, I had a two-hour bus ride with transfers along the way. On that extremely cold December morning, I bundled up and headed for the bus stop. After a long, cold, bus ride, I arrived at my first destination. I filled out forms and waited for hours to be seen. Finally, it was my turn to explain my situation. "I have been drinking for the past twenty-six years. I am ready to do whatever it takes to get sober."

An hour into my story, staff explained that they could not take me. I was referred to other agencies in town. I thought about venturing out into the freezing weather again, but worried that I didn't have enough money to get home. Even with that, I contemplated going back home.

The words, *"You'll be back,"* echoed in my mind.

I told myself that I would never go back, no matter what. It was not a place for anyone to be living—even though I had called it home for six years.

I got on a bus and headed to my next destination. At this site, and even though I came in as an emergency intake, it seemed to take just as long as the first one.

During my breaks from the intake, I went outside to smoke. My last beer from the morning was out of my system. I felt shaky again and began to cry. I noticed a bar next door to the clinic. From my many years as an alcoholic, I knew this bar well. *But then again,* I thought, *what bar didn't I know?* My mind started playing tricks on me. I thought about going to that bar *for just one more drink.*

I never went into that bar; I cannot tell you exactly why. I believe that my prayers, as well as my anger at what my life had become, kept me away. With prayer, hope, and determination, I finally got help.

A clean-and-sober shelter agreed to take me. I had never done anything like this before. I was frightened and on edge. With the bus tickets they gave me, I got on the bus. After an hour passed, I reached the shelter.

At the front door, I buzzed in. A woman met me and welcomed me inside. We walked down a hall and took an elevator to the second floor. I was overwhelmed; it was loud and chaotic. Women were everywhere as they talked and moved about. The television was blaring. I was asked to have a seat by the front desk. With my bag beside me, I sat down. I waited and watched.

A few women must have seen how scared I looked because they sat with me and chatted. To start my intake process, I was taken to a private room where paperwork was placed in front of me. I recall many questions and that a lot of rules were explained to me. I signed all the paperwork even though none of it made any sense to me at the time.

The program was up to each individual to follow. It consisted of rules, bedtimes, shower times, cleaning times, classes, and signatures for completing tasks. I was told how I was expected to behave at all times.

One of the perks to look forward to was a private room if you reached certain levels. But in the beginning, I was placed in a dorm situation. Two bunk beds in each area. My stay would be four months, which was enough time to find treatment and permanent housing. I felt as though I was given a chance at life.

I was grateful. Thankfully, I didn't know what was ahead of me.

The Detox

So my detox began. On the first night, I was already very sick. I was shaking and disoriented. I was aware that detox, without medical treatment, could kill me. At the time, I would have rather died while trying to get sober than live my horrible life anymore as a slave to alcohol.

I don't think I slept more than an hour that first night at the shelter. I was restless and sweat throughout the night. Experiencing severe flulike symptoms, I thought I was going to die. Everything seemed foggy.

The next day, I asked permission to stay in bed as I explained that I was sick with the "flu." This, however, was not a detox center. No one was allowed to detox here for any reason. So I did not tell them that I was detoxing.

I could barely keep fluids down. On the second night, I experienced diarrhea and vomiting. The sweating and body aches continued into the next day. By the third day, I had worsened. I wasn't on a level where I could come and go as I pleased, so I asked for a pass to the hospital. With my pass approved, I got on the bus and headed to the hospital.

On top of detoxing, I was diagnosed with pneumonia. The doctor also told me that I should be on twenty-four hour monitoring while detoxing. After explaining my situation, I humbly declined a hospital stay in fear of losing my spot at the shelter. I was given antibiotics for the pneumonia and a anxiety medication to ease the withdrawals.

Back at the shelter once more, I was allowed bed rest due to the doctor's note. I was very grateful to rest. I remember having overwhelming urges to drink during that first week. Honestly, if I wasn't so sick to go to a bar, I might have. So, my sobriety begins here.

The First Thirty Days

I was shaking and experienced flulike symptoms. My headaches were severe. I walked around in a dreamlike state. Reality was blurred. I was confused all the time. My mind played tricks on me and tried to justify taking a drink. I seemed anxious and couldn't sit still for very long. I had to remind myself constantly why I quit drinking.

I felt as though I was outside my body all the time. I didn't sleep much, and when I did, it wasn't a sound sleep. Noise and light bothered me. I was very angry while fighting the cravings for alcohol.

I continued to read my Bible and pray. I went to five intakes in the first month. I was trying to get into in-patient treatment. The shelter was not a treatment program; it was a place to stay while you got on your feet.

If I had medical insurance, I might have been accepted into a program right away. Without insurance, I was on at least three waiting lists for treatment. As I struggled to get treatment, I ran across an out-patient program. If I met the criteria, the program could take me for free.

After filling out all of the papers, I was soon accepted to a three-month program. Once more, I explained my situation in grave detail and mentioned three months would not be enough for me. After reviewing my case, the program granted me treatment for a year.

I started a program with some of the woman at the shelter. We went to meetings outside the shelter and were expected to get a signature and return promptly. With a sponsor, I started my steps.

The Woman in the Mirror (Part 1)

My life was filled with chaos; I slept my days away.
My nights were filled with drinking; my dreams I drank away.
I didn't recognize myself peering in the mirror.
The last time I checked, I was a little girl.
I guess I'll never know who I might have been.
What books may have I read that might have been my friends?
My memories were robbed and I cannot recall.
My life is one big blur because of alcohol.
If you think you know me, please tell me who I am.
Tell me how I acted and everywhere I've been.
Did I ever smile? Did I ever cry?
Did I have emotions? Did I ever lie?

I've seemed to find sobriety though I struggle every day.
Sometimes all I can do is fold my hands and pray.
My speech is getting better; my words are not so slurred.
Memories are coming back; I'm not a little girl.
The woman in the mirror, I'll have to get to know.
Every day is beautiful without alcohol.

The Woman in the Mirror: (Part 2)

While getting ready one day, I sat on my bed and looked into my handheld mirror. As I saw myself, I was startled and gasped, ''Oh, my!''

The woman in the mirror looked strange to me and not familiar at all. With butterflies in my stomach, I set down the mirror. I felt my face with both hands and wondered if I was dreaming.

I picked the mirror up again; the same thing happened. I looked so old. I had wrinkles around my eyes and on my forehead. My eyes looked grey instead of blue and seemed droopy and hollow. The chin in the mirror didn't resemble my chin at all. My face seemed lifeless; my lips looked grey.

I noticed tiny spider veins around my eyes, cheeks, and chin. *Telltale signs of an alcoholic*, I thought to myself. I panicked and began to cry. *How could I not have noticed these significant changes?*

I thought I looked horrible and probably did. I decided to stay home that day and hoped things would change. I frequented the mirror that day, but nothing had changed. By the next day, I had realized this is how I look. With only days sober, I was shocked to see the real me. I would have to get used to it.

The next day, I went about as usual. I tried to block out the thoughts from yesterday—too scared to recall. I talked about it in group and cried and cried.

I seem to be looking better. Maybe I came to terms with it, or maybe I'm getting used to the woman in the mirror. Whatever the case, I'm getting to know her.

The Second Month

By this point, I was feeling very sad and lonely. My energy was drained, and I was mentally exhausted. The groups and classes, bus rides, and cold weather took its toll on me.

Feeling disoriented and foggy, I still wasn't sleeping well. But I was ecstatic to have made it that far. At the same time, I was overwhelmed and depression set in. Yet, throughout all of this, I was determined to stay sober.

I knew some of the women and staff members fairly well. I was especially fond of a woman in my dorm. I choose to call her Susan. She had the top bunk, and I had the bottom. We exchanged stories and found they were very similar.

Also an alcoholic, Susan struggled with housing problems. We started going on passes together in between our programs and classes. We rode the bus to coffee shops and meetings. We even accompanied one another to some appointments. At times, other women joined us. We had a lot of talks and laughs in the dining area at meal times. We also shared a lot of tears.

Most of the women were encouraging and supportive. Others, it seemed, had simply given up. It was sad to watch.

I looked forward to going back to the shelter after my daily classes. I also started painting nails for the women who couldn't afford a salon. That included almost all of us. With a few volunteers, we had a downstairs room where we could paint nails once a week.

We often painted nails for six hours straight. During that time, we talked, laughed, and cried. All of us looked forward to it each week.

Donations of polish were given to me weekly by staff and women. We never accepted tips as this would defeat the purpose. This time together gave us a chance to get to know one another better. It seemed I was able to put smiles on some faces and on my own.

Third Month

Early in the month, not much had changed. I was still foggy about five days a week and had headaches. I was sleeping a little better, but no big changes. I also had a strange feeling of being misplaced.

One thing, however, seemed better. My cravings for alcohol were slowly subsiding. At this point, people I used to drink with called me—even long distance calls. I either chose not to answer my cell phone or asked them not to call. Most didn't take kindly to this. I was called names and had to block some numbers. I had tried to explain that I wasn't well and couldn't meet up for any reason.

I had told my mother about my plan to get sober as soon as I stepped foot in the shelter. We continued to speak by phone almost every day., I also contacted the rest of my family and let them know where I was. My mother might have been the only one who believed I could stay sober. The rest of my family was hopeful, just hopeful.

I started drawing to pass the time. The women seemed to like my art, so I drew pictures for everyone who asked. It took my mind off things and seemed to relax me. I also began doing some housekeeping jobs, here and there, to support myself.

So, it seemed I might actually stay sober. But, with a pending court case, I let the stress get the best of me. Before I had decided to get sober, I had been in some serious trouble. I knew it was possible that I would face jail time. Still, I tried to assure myself that everything would be fine and that I could get through this without a drink. However, I started losing sleep as the court date got closer and made myself sick with worry.

My housing at the shelter was in jeopardy. I knew if I served more than seven days in jail, the shelter could not hold my bed. I felt as though everything I had worked for was diminishing. I didn't know where I would live. How could I continue treatment if I was locked up?

The thought of losing my newfound support group was more than I could take. I began thinking about drinking more and more. I let my thoughts get the best of me. I had finally earned my first weekend pass. Still, knowing that I would drink, I took my pass. I had given up completely.

The Relapse

I gave in. It seemed that alcohol was the only thing I could turn to. I was throwing away everything I had just learned. I didn't even try to stop myself.

With a one-track mind, I set off to the bar. Once inside, I sat down and ordered a drink. A million things ran through my head. Trying to ignore my thoughts, I grabbed the drink and gulped it down.

Quickly, I ordered another and gulped it down also. I ordered a third drink and headed to the video poker room that I had known all too well. I put a five-dollar bill in the machine and tried to relax. Instead, I started feeling disoriented from the alcohol. As all the feelings started pouring in, I started questioning myself.

It was hard to believe that I was drinking again. Thoughts of family, friends, and sobriety were blocking my drunk. I realized that I wasn't getting any drunker. I couldn't get the euphoric feeling that alcohol once gave me. I couldn't reach the coma state that I had longed for. That was when I realized drinking was not working. It was only making everything worse.

Eventually, I left with an old friend. I decided to go to his house and drink coffee before deciding what to do. I was depressed and lonely. I felt as though I had let everything I had fought for slip away.

I was miserable and knew I didn't want to go down this road again. As morning crept in, I did what needed to be done and face up to the consequences. I called the shelter. I told them what I had done and tried to make amends. I knew this wasn't going to be easy.

According to the shelter's policy, a person was required to have seventy-two hours of sobriety before returning to the shelter. However, I should phone them again, if or when, I did.

I waited out my seventy-two hours. I white-knuckled it and called the shelter again. I told them I managed to stay sober and would like to return. I also told them how bad I felt and that I was willing to accept the consequences for my behavior.

After some contemplation on their part, I was allowed to return. Had I not told them about my relapse, and they found out, I would have not been allowed to return. I was placed on a very low level with new stipulations due to my decision to drink.

I humbly accepted my punishment and struggled to stay sober again. My treatment program also allowed me back after I told them exactly what I had told the shelter. My drinking episode could have cost me my life.

I also reminded myself of what a terrible time I had and realized that alcohol could not solve my problems. Not that it ever did, but I had allowed myself to believe it had helped in the past. Given all that had happened due to my poor judgment during my relapse, I had no reason to believe I would drink again.

Starting Over: Month One

Back at the shelter, I was strict with myself. Consequently, I attended more classes and meetings. Also, because of my relapse, I was shunned by many of the women at the shelter. As human nature has it, the women were quick to judge.

With faith and prayers, I made it back from my first drink to my last in twenty-four hours. I realized how rare this was. Never, at any time, did I take this lightly. And so, my sobriety began again.

Still struggling, my court date arrived. I was sentenced to ten days in jail and probation. I served five days with time served. The shelter had held my bed and allowed me to return. I believe they took into consideration my sheer determination and will to stay sober. My stay was extended another two months given the circumstances of my alcoholism and my willingness to fight.

At the shelter again, I slept better and was able to concentrate. I began focusing solely on recovery. My foggy state had almost disappeared. I started embracing life and learning to live for the first time. I began going for walks, enjoying the outdoors, and seeing things that I had never seen as an isolated alcoholic. My sense of humor stayed intact through it all, and was able to make people laugh. Even though I wasn't always happy, laughing did wonders.

Back in treatment, I became very close to my counselor. She too had struggled with a similar background and understood me. She explained the effects of alcohol and the process an alcoholic must undergo to stay sober.

I attended every group and class that she recommended. As we made decisions together about my treatment plan, I always felt that I had a say in it. She walked me through it every step of the way and helped me with the underlying issues I had that started my drinking early on. She was helping me save my life; I would be forever grateful to her. I never felt that she was just doing her job. I knew she was going that extra mile for me. Maybe she saw a little glint of herself in me, or maybe she knew I could stay sober. Whatever the case, I felt that she sincerely cared.

I attended five classes a weekin treatment outside the shelter and attended some classes at the shelter. My mom and I enjoyed Bible study over the phone. I continued my programs and step work with my sponsor. My plate was full and that's what it took for me to stay sober. Finally, everything began to come together. I also realized that this would be a lifetime commitment.

Last Month at the Shelter

As my time was coming to an end at the shelter, I was on waiting lists for subsidized housing. I was accepted into a new program that allowed me a place to live while finishing treatment. It wasn't too far from the shelter, so I could come back to visit. I didn't know much about the new program, but they accepted me. It was time to move.

Also, this was the point at which I made the time to make my amends to my children and family. I would make amends to those I had upset along my path. Most likely, I will never be able to reach everyone, but I won't give up trying.

With a many mixed emotions, I was sad to be leaving the shelter. I had felt comfortable there. Now, I was very fearful of leaving. I said my good-byes to those I had been close to me. I also left my phone number with a few of the women and promised to stay in touch.

As a new journey awaited me, I was excited for something new. I also felt as if I was getting to become the person I had always wanted to be. My determination seemed to be stronger than ever. I didn't know how rough things would get and was glad I hadn't.

The Move and Beyond
(Three to Eight Months)

I filled out the paperwork for a new room. Like the shelter, following the rules played a crucial part in my three-month stay. Extensions were granted to those who followed the program.

I met with my floor counselor, who explained the basics to me. She had a small office on my floor with the hours posted for when she could be reached. Signatures for meetings and classes were expected here. Random urine analysis (UA) tests were given here.

My new room was on the third floor wasn't what I expected. I'm not sure what I expected, but this wasn't it. The room was eight feet by five feet. My bedroom window overlooked a bar across the street. Someone said if we could stay sober here, we could stay sober anywhere. The room had a twin bed, a desk, a chair, a small sink and mirror, a mini fridge, and shelves opposing the bed. I humbled myself and was thankful for having a roof over my head.

I could have stayed with family, but I declined to ask for help. I got myself here, and I needed to get myself well. It seemed I had everything I needed. When I found out this was a coed building, I knew it would be hard to adjust. The bedroom door was heavy and had a solid dead bolt. It made me feel safe at the time.

I had to sign in and out every day as I came and went. I was to leave my key at the front desk when leaving and pick it up upon my return. A 10:00 p.m. curfew was placed on me, but I was used to curfews from living at the shelter. We shared bathrooms, showers, and kitchen. Each floor held its own specific program.

Also, outsiders had no access to the elevators or stairs. The six floors were monitored by front desk staff, cameras, and daily floor checks. For safety reasons, we were not allowed to frequent other floors. Visitors had to sign in and out with valid identification during specific times.

Inside my room, the initial rules and move, wore off. Suddenly, I felt lonely, very lonely. Once I unpacked my boxes, I cried. I didn't know anyone here. I missed my friends, especially Susan, at the shelter. When I called my family, their reassurance helped me get through the first three days.

I often ate food that didn't need to be cooked, so I wouldn't have to go to the kitchen. At other times, I used the microwave that I had purchased while I was at the shelter. Everyone seemed to congregate in the kitchen area, so I tried to avoid it completely. I used the bathroom and shower across the hall from my room and stayed pretty stationary.

By the end of the third day, I had met a few of my neighbors. Some knocked on my door to welcome me or caught me in the hall. Most were male. They seemed sincere in telling me not to hesitate if I needed anything. The fourth floor held approximately thirty people with only seven females, including myself.

As cabin fever was beginning to set it, I decided to venture out. I left my key and went outside. Never had I ever seen so many bars and taverns in such a small radius.

Later, I learned we were living in the middle of entertainment central. The police blocked off the streets on weekend nights as mobs of partyers barhopped and filled the streets. Very loud music filled our building from 10:00 p.m. until 2:30 a.m. on the weekends.

Although, I could witness the arrests by police, I tried not to watch as the bloody faces and screams made me sad. I never thought I would get used to this, but I did.

People often filmed the arrests with their cell phones, while the police tried to block this by using tarps and barricades. I was thankful to be on the other side of this insanity for once. It broke my heart. I walked around for blocks and encountered bar after bar. I knew I was going to have to handle all of this. I just wasn't sure how.

Making my way back to the convenience store on the corner I bought some snacks. I spoke to some people outside and learned that meetings were held in the basement seven days a week. Someone told me that I didn't need to worry that the meetings were a recovery message.

I was invited to attend a meeting in the basement of my building that evening. Not knowing anyone, I felt out of place. But everyone seemed friendly, and I chatted with a few people after the meeting. I also recognized a few faces from other meetings I had attended while at the shelter. So, that is how my stay on the fourth floor began.

Within the first few weeks, I was attending my outside treatment again. I had a taken a few weeks off to move and get settled. During that time, I also met two women in my hall. One was very kind and soft spoken; I choose to call her Mary. Her addiction had brought her to this point in recovery. We spoke of our pasts and our journeys. After hearing Mary's story, mine didn't seem harsh at all. As we shared so many feelings and emotions, we bonded quickly as we shared our fears and concerns.

We agreed that a coed building was of some concern to us. Mary shared stories of inappropriate actions that happened before I arrived. She warned me of those who I should avoid. And for that, I was grateful.

I was surrounded by a lot of people, just like myself, who were broken and damaged. Among other things, I didn't possess good communication skills. So I knew this situation could get rough.

After a few months passed, I began to know people and had my hand in the kitchen. I made some friends and quickly became a presence on the floor. I let it be known that I was here to stay until I finished treatment. I also stressed that I was serious about treatment and my recovery.

I missed Susan from the shelter. For the most part, her phone was not on. Although we didn't speak much anymore, she did visit once, but it wasn't the same. Other than an occasional run in, I no longer saw her. At times, however, I did see some of the women from the shelter. I ran into them on the bus and at other meetings around town. It seemed we all went our separate ways.

I began spending a lot of time with Mary as we had coffee together every morning. Both of us had coffee makers in our rooms, so we took turns making it. Whenever possible, we also shared cooking and eating our meals together. We talked a lot about our pasts and what had brought us to our addictions. We shared what we learned from our separate treatment programs. She was just as determined as I was to stay sober.

As time went on, we became closer. We ventured out together to meetings, malls, walks, and coffee shops. We watched a lot of movies together on my laptop or her computer. That was probably our favorite pastime. Mary and I chatted most mornings and evenings.

Still, things began to get rough for both of us. Not long into my stay on the fourth floor, things began to change. A group of males on the floor started roaming the halls together. Somehow, they believed they owned the entire floor. Even though they didn't have a room in our hallway and weren't supposed to be in our hallway, they roamed the hallway anyway.

Of course, this occurred only when the counselors had left for the day. As reluctant as I am to discuss other addict's behaviors, this was a part of my journey. I must relate what I experienced.

At the time, many people on my floor had been recently released from different prisons around the state. Fights and arguments amongst the people occurred on my floor daily. Some were threatened. Some females, including myself, were sexually harassed.

When my concerns were not heard by my fourth-floor counselor, I went over her head. I wrote two of the males up for their behavior toward me. Myself and one of the men were asked to meet up in the kitchen with staff present to discuss the situation. As the men denied the harassment allegations, nothing was done.

My tears turned to rain. Because I had written them up, they were out for vengeance. The men got off scot-free, and knew it. They decided to make my stay a living hell—and they did. They threw things at me, pushed me, and screamed at me. I was called horrible names, many of which I didn't understand. They continued to sexually harass me weekly.

Mary endured similar treatment from these men. At least two other women on the floor admitted to the same harassment. I tried to hold my ground, but there were too many men.

Was this something I must endure to change my life in the long run? I wondered as I cried every day. I was harassed while coming or going from my room. This group of males even threatened me outside the building with witnesses present.

But heads turned away while this was happening—probably for fear of the same treatment. Mostly, I blamed myself for being in this situation. One day, I couldn't take it anymore. Instead of hiding in my room, I confronted them head on. I called them names and threatened them. I started acting out and treating them the way they had treated me.

Of course, that didn't work. It only made the situation worse. So I started avoiding them all together again. After months of enduring this, one of the men was picked up for shoplifting. Another relapsed and was kicked out. Very slowly and one-by-one, each of the men disappeared.

While all this was happening, our female counselor took a new job. Her replacement was a male counselor who was said to have had fifteen years sober. He seemed sincere and seemed to be cleaning up the floor. But things soon became weird again. His door remained closed during office hours while we could clearly hear him.

When I talked to him, he didn't seem to make any sense at all. He often nodded off while I was checking in with him. Mary noticed the same thing. But the floor was better, so we ignored his behaviors. Soon, he was gone. A lot of talk circulated that he had relapsed, but it really wasn't any of my business. Once again, we were without a floor manager, which was my only concern at the time.

Through the tough patches, Mary and I remained close. We continued to have coffee. And whenever possible, we tried to come and go together. We remained friends through it all.

As things were getting back to normal, I started feeling better, safer, and back on track. I managed to graduate from out-patient treatment. With my certificates in hand, I felt as though I had accomplished so much. I was proud of myself for making it this far.

Nine to Eleven Months

On a waiting list, I was transferred to the fourth floor, which was the employment readiness floor. My new room was a bit larger. I bought curtains at a secondhand store and a few knickknacks to pretty up my room. I had a beautiful, soft, pink blanket. It was much bigger than my bed, but I folded it in half and made it work. I also acquired a soft, pink rug for my floor. I lined my shelves with used material that I bought. Everything was in order, neat, and clean. As I turned this room into a safe haven for myself, I began to love it here.

It was summer again and beautiful. I loved the sunshine. Born and raised here, it was always green and beautiful. Although I had been cleaning RVs, the job was seasonal and would end soon. I was looking forward to moving upstairs and to full-time employment. During this time, I wrote a lot of papers for treatment. Finally, I felt as though I could stand on my own two feet.

I was also painting and drawing. Some of my art was shown at an art gallery. This opportunity arose from the program I was in. For that opportunity, I was very thankful.

Now, and on the fourth floor, I finally started healing. Things started falling into place. This floor was different. People worked, came home, and cooked meals. Although these people struggled, they were very goal oriented. I also met the floor manager. He was strict to say the least. At the same time, he was a very caring and understanding man.

I felt he understood me and that I was safe. As I already knew some of the people on this floor, I felt very comfortable. When my cleaning job ended, I started working on my resume, attire, and the job search from Monday through Friday.

This entailed a lot of walking and many bus rides. My chance at a halfway normal life was underway. I also was getting to know a lot of the people here. Spending a lot of time together I became close with some. My friend, Mary, came to visit often, and I also went to see her. We met up whenever possible for a meeting and coffee.

Living a few blocks from the waterfront, Mary and I spent a lot of time there. We also joined other people from the program to visit parks, malls, and the downtown square. Sometimes on weekends, we brought lunches and sat at the waterfront and talked. All and all, I was getting out a lot with many different people from the program. I'd tell my story and listen to what brought many of them here. We were all getting to know each other.

Twelve to Fifteen Months

After a lot of hard work and applications, I finally landed a job in telemarketing. It wasn't my ideal job, but I didn't care. I was happy to be working. As in everything else, I gave it my all. And, at this point, I began a relationship with Lewis, a man I had known for thirteen years.

Lewis had never been a drinker or addict of any kind. And, he had dealt with me in my dinking days. In the past, we seemed to get along even when I was at my worst. He always treated me with kindness, and I did the same. Lewis and I were very close; he had been with me through a lot of my struggles. Lewis knew my story well and always chose to look beyond the alcoholic in me. Slowly, we began dating.

We dated and had a lot of fun together. Lewis also listened as I poured out my heart about the struggles I had recently been through and was still facing. Lewis expressed his happiness in seeing me sober. His comfort and warmth was something I had never experienced. He always seemed to say the right thing to me. I began to feel something that I had never felt before. Someone loved me and didn't want anything other than love in return. I couldn't wait to talk to him and see him. His arms and his soft words made me feel alive. Lewis, too, expressed his want to see me as much as possible. So we talked on the phone a lot and saw each other when we could. I continued working and struggled with that.

I had become close to a lot of people on my floor. We laughed and helped one another with our struggles. Almost everyone on the fourth floor seemed to get along well. Still, there were a few trouble makers on the floor, but they didn't make it long.

At work, we had daily quotas to reach. So, my job could be on the chopping block at the end of each day. I patiently waited to see if mt boss needed me the next day. This took a toll on me. The stress was a lot to handle. I didn't know if I would have a job the next day or not. I started making my quotas, but things didn't change. I still stood at my boss's desk, like a little kid in trouble, every evening after work. I waited to see if I had a job for the next day.

After a month of this, I was really sick. I believe it was due to stress. I continued to show up for work even though I felt terrible. I ended up in the hospital for minor surgery. Even with a doctor's notes, I was let go.

I had put up with so much stress, but I wasn't going to allow this. I called the head of the company and explained what I had been through. I told him how hard I had worked and wanted to keep my job even though child support took 70 percent from each of my checks. The rest went toward rent to my program. He told me to take a week off to heal and return to work.

As you can imagine, my boss was not too happy with me when I returned to work. He was angry that I went above his head. Others in the office told me how badly he spoke about me. It also showed in the way he treated me. But I kept on working while undergoing stress.

Lewis and I spoke about my moving in with him. However, he lived outside the city and about an hour from where I was. It would have been difficult to commute back and forth to work from his house, so we declined. I told him I would like to stick with the job and stay in the program for awhile longer.

As I continued working and time went on, things got worse at work. Again, Lewis and I discussed the idea of my moving in with him. He owned properties and could use my help painting and cleaning his units. Having worked with him in the past here and there, I knew we would work well together.

So it seemed like moving in with him was for the best. I discussed it with my program, sponsor, and family. All seemed to be in agreement about my move. I was feeling anxious to be leaving the program, but I also knew I couldn't stay forever. So, once again, I said my good-byes and promised to keep in touch with some of the people from the fourth floor.

Sixteen to Twenty Months

I began to live life on the outside. No curfews, program managers, signatures, and urine analyses. At first, things seemed to be going well as I settled in. My friend, Mary, visited occasionally and spent the night. We would watch movies and catch up on one another's current lives.

Lewis welcomed Mary into our home and hosted us while we caught up. He seemed intrigued by our struggles and what we had overcome. Somehow, I felt as though Mary and I had an unbreakable bond. I always looked forward to her visits. After settling in, I began to get busy.

Lewis and I had a lot of work in front of us. First, we began cleaning up the house room by room. The house had been let go a little since Lewis hadn't had help for some time. Things started off well, and the time we spent together was wonderful.

Lewis and I shared so much with each other. We made goals to accomplish and started working on them right away. The first month was great amid a lot of laughs. Soon after the first month, things begin to change.

We realized I may have moved in too soon and wasn't ready. While I had a lot more time here to myself, it seemed as though he expected a lot of my free time to be spent with him. Because I had been in a room by myself for so long, I was not used to having anyone around. Sharing space was difficult for me. I also realized a lot more changes were in store for me. Because we couldn't seem to agree on many things, I returned to counseling again.

I joined groups as well as mental health and addiction counseling. I explained that I was living outside of the programs and needed new skills to cope. I added that my boyfriend also saw some needed changes in himself. We worked together on everything. From bedtimes to the way we approached one another in heated discussions. It was hard for me to admit my faults and fix them.

Still, we never let things get out of hand in our disagreements. At times, however, we walked away for a breather. We never threw things, hit things, or slammed doors. We never thought about physical violence for any reason. We were never that upset.

My past relationships often became very physical. So not feeling the anger that I had before was empowering. I never felt upset to that point with Lewis. I realized that I was having a normal relationship. Life has its ups and downs. And without alcohol, things didn't get out of control. So we began to make changes throughout our relationship.

We set aside time for ourselves without distractions of the outside world. We needed time to get to know one another's likes and dislikes. We set goals and carried them out. We practiced patience and respect with one another.

Lewis taught me a lot about life and learning what it meant to be a couple. I was learning how to budget and pay bills on time. I managed stress better and better as time went on. I also learned math and some computer skills as well as gardening and outdoor skills.

I taught Lewis to paint and draw. Together, both of us were learning new things. I helped Lewis let his guard down and become silly with me on occasion. Both of us began to come out from behind the walls we had put up in front of us. We did fun and interesting things together. I began enjoying the outdoors more and more. We were laughing, loving, and enjoying life.

Although things were rocky in the beginning, we made changes and pulled through. I'm grateful that we made the necessary changes. It was well worth the hard work. Things were coming together as we were falling in love. With twenty months into sobriety, life was going well.

When I Finally Met Myself

At twenty months sober, I greeted myself with a hello. I had so many questions for myself. How did I stay sober this long? What made me finally get sober and quit sabotaging myself?

I spoke to myself in a quiet tone. It seemed that I possessed the tools to survive. While seemingly confident, I still had a glint of fright in my eyes and a fear of relapse. Thinking upon my past, I remembered where I had come from. Never wanting to return, I reminded myself of the destructive path I had walked along. I told myself stories about my childhood and my shattered dreams. Nighttime scared me and daytime never existed. I remembered past relationships and the daily battles with drinking.

The memories of shaking, headaches, and complete exhaustion jolted me. I was reminded of my inability to speak or walk at times. I was reminded of the severe loss of my children. I reminded myself of the jails and institutions where I had lived. I reminded myself of who I was today and all I had accomplished.

I am no different from any other addict or alcoholic. My story is not different from any other addict or alcoholic. I kept journals and logs of my journey into sobriety. I needed the memories on paper in case I ever forgot.

So, I changed pace and told myself of the sunshine and new journeys that awaited me. I let my past begin to fade away. I needed to look ahead and focus on the goals I had set before me. And, I reminded myself never to forget my past totally because it kept me sober.

I remind myself about the people I met on my journey and the comfort and understanding that they gave me. Of all the stories that I heard and all the tears that were shed, it was the prayers that kept me sober and the rooms kept me safe. Meeting myself, at twenty months sober, was incredible. Walking down this new path was a dream come true.

Twenty through Twenty-Three Months

I'm so new in sobriety, yet I've learned so much. It's hard to believe I've come this far. Still in counseling, I was getting close to graduating again. I am grateful for so much. I am grateful for my children, family, friends, and Lewis.

I know it has been a long, hard road into sobriety. Without these struggles and learning experiences, I might not have changed. The trials are what made me strong.

I never thought of myself as someone who could finish anything. Yet, I have accomplished many things at once. I finally cleaned up the wreckage of my past.

I was doing what I could to take care of court fines, child support, medical bills, and school loans. Some of these looked impossible to pay off, but slowly I had a handle on them. It will take years for me to make a dent in all of these bills. I will not give up until they have been paid.

At times, I have had occasional cravings for alcohol, but these became less and less frequent. It became easier to deal with the cravings when they arose. And I continue to work beside Lewis.

I still work on my past as I move forward. I am not quite where I want to be, but I have come so far. I am living life today and continued helping those I could.

When offered the opportunity to do some volunteer work, I jumped at the chance. Our local animal shelter needed foster homes for cats. I had frequented the shelter looking for a kitten of my own. However, I was offered a pregnant, adult cat. I would keep her and the kittens until the kittens reached the age of eight weeks. At that point, I took the mother cat and her kittens back to the shelter to be adopted. I kept one of the kittens. Feeding, playing and loving a cat can be so rewarding..

I have more plans. Lewis also coaches softball, so I joined for my first softball season. Mary is still a part of my life; I hope that never changes. Today, I look forward to life and have a clear picture of what I can make of it. I know how far I can go if I continue to fight the horrible disease of alcoholism.

Post-Acute Withdrawal Syndrome

About five days before taking my two years clean and sober, I started feeling strange. I was experiencing the post-acute withdrawal syndrome often called PAWS. I was aware that PAWS often occurred close to milestones in sobriety. I had experienced this syndrome in the past, but I never recognized what it was until I was in tears. Every time it hits, it feels as though my whole world has turned upside down.

This time, I didn't recognize what it was until I was about to give up on everything. Overly emotional and overly sensitive, I felt as though no one cared.

I cancelled Bible study and didn't feel like getting out of bed. I tossed and turned, but I couldn't seem to rest. I was aggravated and felt detached from everything. Little things annoyed me, and I was extremely irritable.

When I became argumentative with others, I questioned my sobriety and wondered if I might not make it. As thoughts of drinking consumed my mind, I went to the computer and pulled up information about PAWS. The article described exactly what I was going through. I was on an emotional rollercoaster. The symptoms lasted a very, very, long two weeks.

From the information and tips that I read about PAWS, I learned this could occur again, but now I knew I could get through it. Still, PAWS catches me off guard.

I recommend anyone struggling with sobriety to read about PAWS. For me, knowing about it is half the battle.

Twenty-Four months

On March 13, 2015, I took two years clean and sober. Still feeling a bit disoriented, I was not quite over the rollercoaster of emotions. Somehow, I managed to pull it together.

Bob took me out for lunch and coffee to reflect on my two years. I did some journaling and reflected on how I got this far. While I had expected to have accomplished more by now, I knew it takes time. I will continue to put sobriety first in my life and let the rest fall in place.

I also knew that more struggles are on their way. While I am aware that life is not a bowl of cherries, I have had and will have times when I feel like giving up. But I choose to fight instead of giving up. I know this from the many times I've had to fight for my sobriety. It is my hope that when I'm feeling better, I can take a short trip to celebrate on reaching my two-year mark in recovery. For now, I'm happy to have made it this far. I'm grateful for what I have and who I am today.

The Chopsticks

Early in sobriety, I started making hair sticks from ordinary chopsticks to hold up my hair. The process is quite long. First, I carefully inspect each pair of chopsticks and look for splinters, nicks, holes, and cracks. After the defects are fixed, I paint the chopsticks. Next, I sand and file away all the flaws. Sometimes, the chopsticks are cracked almost in half.

These take more time as I have to glue them first. I think all of the chopsticks are worth fixing. Once I have fixed, sanded, and filed them, I begin painting. Using various colors, I make different colored rings on the tips. Sometimes, I use sparkles and gloss to make the chopsticks shine.

In the end, I have beautiful and seemingly flawless hair sticks. In a sense, we are all chopsticks in recovery. Some of us just need a little work. Some of us are severely broken and require extra work. With the proper tools and steps, eventually all of us can be fixed. By inspecting ourselves, we can determine how long this process might take. Each of us is different. In the end, my hair sticks are all very beautiful and unique—just like me and you.

The Garden

Free from prison of alcohol, I now have insight instead of seeing. Today, I have a garden that takes seeds, tools, and a lot of hard work to make it grow.

To start my garden, I planted determination and hope. Then I watered my first seeds often and watched them sprout. Later, I planted dignity and courage as I carefully watched over them.

As time went on, my garden seemed small. So, I started planting a lot of seeds all at once.

Peace and love were my favorite plants to grow. I made a special place to plant my spiritual garden. I planted patience, kindness, and goodness in the same row to keep them together. Then I planted faith and joy next to them.

When it came time to plant self-control and mildness, I cried. I wasn't sure that they would grow. But just recently, they too started to sprout. Needing a water source, I ran a river right through the middle of my garden. The river included my family, support system, and spiritual program. I needed sunshine too, so I sprinkled gratitude over the entire garden.

As my garden begun to flourish, I needed to cultivate it. So I began gathering the appropriate tools. Emotional wellness came first. Next, I gathered optimism, trust, and self-confidence. These tools were a must. But I needed social tools as well, so I picked up compassion and learned how to be supportive and good natured. When it came time to gather my intellectual tools, I realized I already owned them. These included common sense, creativity, and curiosity.

I realize more storms will come along the way. These may cause me to replant, reseed, and rewater my garden.

Awareness of the storms ahead will be the key to my success.

Today, at two and a one-half years sober, I believe I have the determination to make my garden everything I had dreamed and hoped it would be.

The Aftercare

I will have many more seeds to plant and many more tools to gather along the way. If my garden is going to continue to flourish, I need to care for it as I do now.

I will be planting independence and self-acceptance in the near future. I will watch for storms and take cover as necessary. I will hold all of these plants and tools close to my heart as I learn to love myself.

People can change and they do. I know, because I did.

Made in the USA
San Bernardino, CA
13 December 2015